GEORGIA

GEORGIA

THEN & NOW

Prepared by
Geography Department

Lerner Publications Company
Minneapolis

Series editors: Mary M. Rodgers, Tom Streissguth,
  Colleen Sexton
Photo researcher: Kathy Raskob
Designer: Zachary Marell

Our thanks to the following for their help in preparing
and checking the text of this book: Dr. Craig ZumBrunnen,
Department of Geography, University of Washington;
Dr. Melor Sturua, Hubert H. Humphrey Institute of Public
Affairs; Sergey and Karen Chernyaev.

Terms in **bold** appear in a glossary that starts on page 52.

Pronunciation Guide

Abkhazia	ahb-kha-zeh-ah
Adjara	ah-tcha-rah
Akhaltsikhe	ah-khal-tsee-khee
glasnost	GLAZ-nost
Mtskheta	msket-ah
perestroika	pehr-eh-STROY-kah
Shevardnadze	sheh-vard-nads-eh
Shiite	SHEE-iyt
Tbilisi	tbee-lee-see
Tkibuli	tkee-buh-lee
Tkvarcheli	tkvar-cheh-lee
Tskhenis	sken-ihs
Tskhali	ska-lee
Tskhinvali	skin-vah-lee

LIBRARY OF CONGRESS CATALOGING-IN-PUBLICATION DATA

Georgia / prepared by Geography Department, Lerner Publica-
tions Company.
    p.   cm.—(Then & now)
  Includes index.
  Summary: Discusses the geography, history, politics, economics,
and ecology of the former Soviet republic of Georgia.
  ISBN 0-8225-2807-X (lib. bdg.)
  1. Georgia (Republic)—Juvenile literature. [1. Georgia (Republic)]
I. Lerner Publications Company. Geography Dept. II. Series:
Then & now   (Minneapolis, Minn.)
DK675.6.G46   1993
947'.95—dc20   93-19291
                                             CIP
                                             AC

Manufactured in the United States of America
1 2 3 4 5 6 – I/JR – 98 97 96 95 94 93

INTRODUCTION • 7

CHAPTER ONE
The Land and People of Georgia • 11

CHAPTER TWO
Georgia's Story • 25

CHAPTER THREE
Making a Living in Georgia • 41

CHAPTER FOUR
What's Next for Georgia? • 49

GLOSSARY • 52

INDEX • 55

A vendor sells fresh strawberries at an open-air market.

"I cannot allow the country to be torn apart."

Eduard Shevardnadze

In 1992, the Soviet Union would have celebrated the 75th anniversary of the revolution of 1917. During that revolt, political activists called **Communists** overthrew the czar (ruler) and the government of the **Russian Empire.** The revolution of 1917 was the first step in establishing the 15-member **Union of Soviet Socialist Republics (USSR).**

The Soviet Union stretched from eastern Europe across northern Asia and contained nearly 300 million people. Within this vast nation, the Communist government guaranteed housing, education, health care, and lifetime employment. Communist leaders told farmers and factory workers that Soviet citizens owned all property in common. The new nation quickly **industrialized,** meaning it built many new factories and upgraded existing ones. It also modernized and enlarged its farms. In addition, the USSR created a huge, well-equipped military force that allowed it to become one of the most powerful nations in the world.

People crowd the streets of the capital city of Tbilisi during a pro-independence rally. Some demonstrators carry the flag used by Georgia from 1918 to 1921—a period when the republic was a self-ruling state.

(Left) **In 1992, refugees fled their destroyed homes near Tkvarcheli, a mining town in the Georgian province of Abkhazia. Since fighting broke out in this northwestern region in the late 1980s, more than 80,000 people have relocated.** (Below) **An archway offers a view of old church ruins. Georgians accepted the Christian faith in the 4th century** A.D.

By the early 1990s, the Soviet Union was in a period of rapid change and turmoil. The central government had mismanaged the economy, which was failing to provide goods. To control the various ethnic groups within the USSR, the Communists had long restricted many freedoms. People throughout the vast nation were dissatisfied.

Georgia, a small republic in the southwestern Soviet Union, declared its independence from Soviet rule in 1990. After the declaration, riots, violent demonstrations, and other confrontations within the new nation pointed to the possibility of all-out civil war.

The developments in Georgia and elsewhere in the USSR worried some old-style Communists. In August 1991, these conservative Communists tried to use Soviet military power to overthrow the nation's president, Mikhail Gorbachev. Their effort failed and hastened the breakup of the USSR.

After the Soviet collapse, conditions in Georgia became even more unstable. Georgian president Zviad Gamsakhurdia had enacted laws and had authorized arrests that divided the Georgian government. In response, demonstrators fought with police and demanded Gamsakhurdia's resignation. After a siege of the Georgian parliament by anti-Gamsakhurdia activists, the president fled the country. A state council ruled until October 1992, when national elections brought Eduard Shevardnadze, an ally of Gorbachev, to power as Georgia's leader.

Although one of the first Soviet republics to declare its independence, Georgia was the last to gain admission to the **United Nations.** The new Georgian republic has so far not joined the **Commonwealth of Independent States**, a loose association of members of the old USSR.

With a new government in place, Georgia is turning to its many pressing economic and social problems. Ethnic violence mars relations between Georgians, and the country's economy is in a shambles. It remains to be seen what Shevardnadze and his colleagues can do to resolve internal rivalries and to put Georgia on the road to economic and political recovery.

*The posture of **Mother Georgia**, a statue in Tbilisi, reveals two aspects of the Georgian character. The sword in the figure's right hand is reserved for Georgia's enemies, while the wine goblet held in her left hand is only for Georgia's friends.*

CHAPTER ONE

The Land and People of Georgia

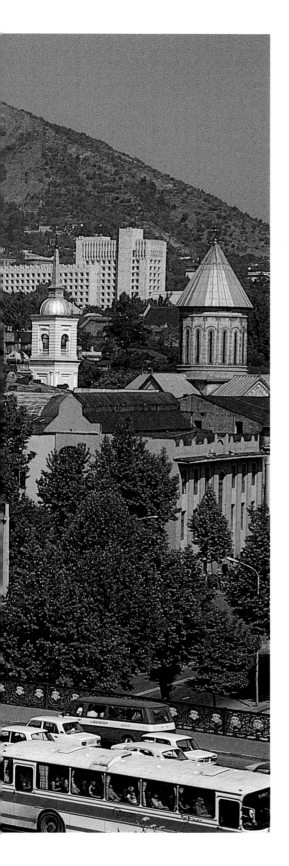

L ying in southwestern Asia, the Republic of Georgia is a rugged land with a strongly nationalistic people. In fact, **ethnic Georgians** refer to themselves as Kartvelians, and they call their homeland Sakartvelo. These references are related to Kartli, an early Georgian kingdom. The name *Georgia* may come from a Greek word meaning ''people who work the earth'' or from *Gurj,* the name the ancient Persians (modern Iranians) gave to the inhabitants of Georgia.

Georgia covers 26,911 square miles (69,699 square kilometers), an area about the size of Ireland or the state of West Virginia. Western Georgia curves around the eastern shore of the Black Sea. The ridge line of the Greater Caucasus Mountains forms Georgia's long northern border with Russia. Georgia also has a short southern frontier with Turkey.

The former Soviet republics of Armenia and Azerbaijan lie to the south and east, respectively. Because the Caucasus Mountains cross Georgia,

Founded in the 5th century A.D., *Tbilisi exhibits Georgian, Arab, Byzantine, Russian, and Soviet architectural styles. The name* Tbilisi *comes from the Georgian word for ''warm'' and refers to the city's many heated mineral springs.*

(Left) **A full moon rises over the snow-dusted peaks of the Greater Caucasus Mountains of northern Georgia.** (Below) **In South Ossetia—a former Georgian province that seeks to unite with North Ossetia in Russia—a member of the national guard shoulders her weapon. Warfare has killed about 1,500 people and has leveled many Ossetian villages in the region.**

Armenia, and Azerbaijan, these three states are sometimes together referred to as the **Transcaucasian republics.**

Within the boundaries of Georgia are Adjara, Abkhazia, and South Ossetia. The last two areas experienced civil unrest during the early 1990s. Located in the northwest between Russia and the Black Sea, Abkhazia has been fighting for independence from Georgia. Self-rule is also the goal of South Ossetia, a former Georgian province that was abolished by Georgia's parliament in 1990. South Ossetia wants to unite with North Ossetia, which is part of Russia but is located on the north side of the Greater Caucasus. By comparison, Adjara—in southwestern Georgia—has been politically quiet.

• The Lay of the Land •

About 85 percent of Georgia's territory is mountainous. In the north, defining the shape of the Russian border, are the Greater Caucasus Mountains, whose peaks reach more than 16,500 feet (5,029 meters) above sea level. The Lesser Caucasus Mountains rise to a height of about 10,000 feet (3,048 m) in southern Georgia. The lower Suram range stretches from north to south, linking the two taller mountain chains and separating western and eastern Georgia.

In western Georgia is the Colchis Lowland, a flat, marshy area that was once covered by the Black Sea. Named for an ancient Georgian kingdom, the lowland receives the alluvial sediments carried by the Rioni, Inguri, and Kodori rivers. Productive soil and artificial drainage projects have made most of the lowland suitable for raising high-value crops, such as tea, tobacco, and citrus fruits.

Nearly surrounded by mountains, the Kartalinian Plain dominates a high plateau in central Georgia between the cities of Khashuri and Mtskheta. Loess, a particularly fertile soil, covers the plain, which supports citrus fruit trees, grape vineyards, and dairy farms. Farther east, the land features broad stretches of arid steppes (grasslands) that must be irrigated to be farmed.

Earthquakes have struck Georgia throughout its history. The most recent serious tremor took place in 1991 and ruined many houses and farm buildings.

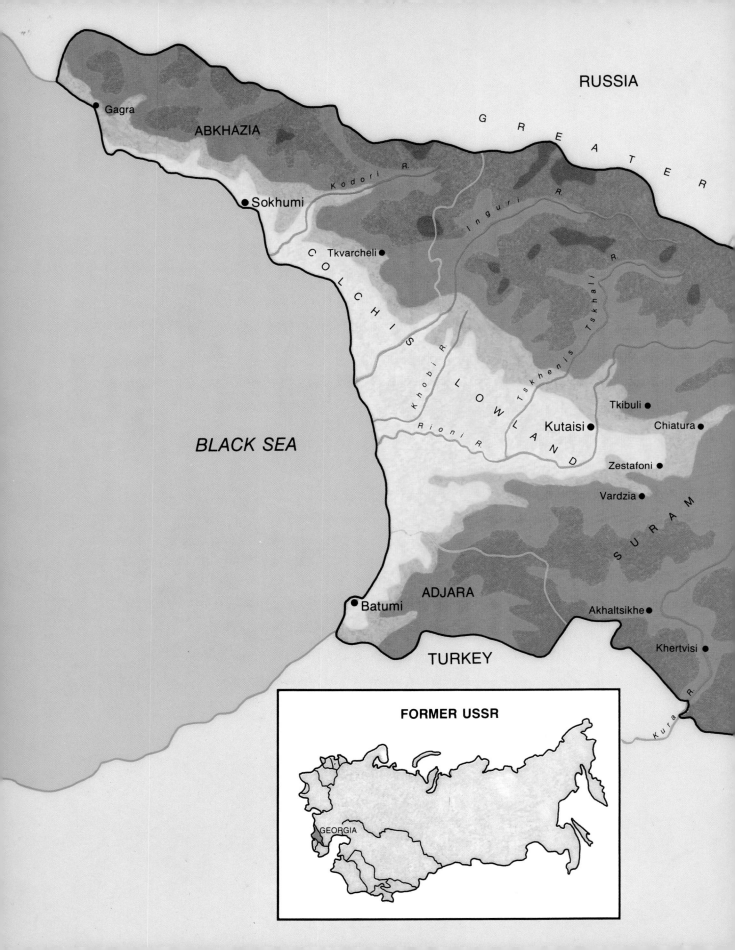

RUSSIA

● Gagra

ABKHAZIA

Kodori R.

Inguri R.

GREATER

● Sokhumi

C O L C H I S

● Tkvarcheli ●

Khobi R.

Rioni R.

Tskhenis Tskhali R.

L O W L A N D

Tkibuli ●

Kutaisi ●

Chiatura ●

Zestafoni ●

Vardzia ●

S U R A M

BLACK SEA

ADJARA

● Batumi

Akhaltsikhe ●

Khertvisi ●

Kura R.

TURKEY

FORMER USSR

GEORGIA

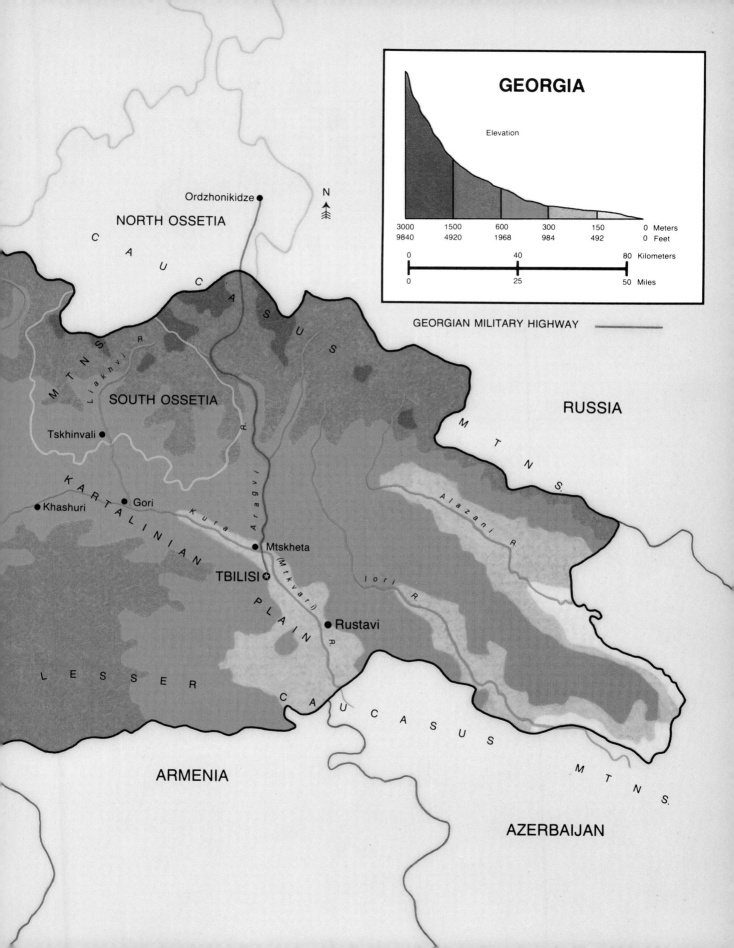

• *Rivers* •

Georgia's many short rivers begin in the mountains and continue either westward to the Black Sea or eastward to the Caspian Sea. These fast-running waterways are important sources of hydroelectricity and irrigation.

Western Georgia has a highly developed river system, which is dominated by the Rioni River. Rising in the Greater Caucasus, the Rioni flows for 179 miles (288 km) before reaching the Black Sea near the port of Poti. Boats can travel upstream as far as the city of Kutaisi, where major hydroelectric stations operate. The great flow of the river also brings huge deposits of alluvial soil to Poti, whose shoreline pushes farther into the sea every year. Other rivers in the region include the Inguri, the Kodori, the Khobi, and the Tskhenis Tskhali, which is a tributary of the Rioni.

The Kura River and its tributaries—including the Liakhvi, the Aragvi, the Iori, and the Alazani—irrigate

(Above) *Heavy with sediment, the Kura River, which Georgians call the Mtkvari, winds through Tbilisi.* (Below) *Young Georgians lift their skirts to enjoy the waters of the Black Sea at Batumi, a major Georgian port.*

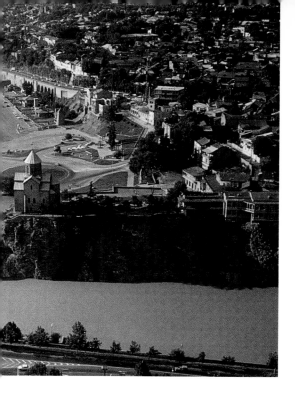

the farmland of the Kartalinian Plain. Rising in Turkey, the Kura crosses the border into Georgia near the town of Khertvisi and is then called the Mtkvari by Georgians. Mountain streams swell the river as it curves eastward toward Tbilisi, the Georgian capital. As the river increases in volume, dams harness its current and convert it into hydroelectric power for Georgian cities and industries. The longest river of the Caucasus region, the Kura eventually passes through Azerbaijan before emptying into the Caspian Sea.

• Climate •

Georgia's diverse climate includes the wet subtropical west, the dry steppes of the southeast, and the chilly Greater Caucasus Mountains. This tall chain shields much of the country from cold air blowing southward from the plains of Russia. As a result, Georgia has a much warmer climate than do neighboring states that lie along the same latitude.

The greatest influence on the climate of Georgia is the Black Sea, whose warm, moist air masses bathe the Colchis Lowland and reach as far east as the Suram Mountains. Winters in the west are rainy and warm, and summers are humid. The Caucasus region, in contrast, experiences cold, wet winters and cool summers. Above 11,500 feet (3,505 m), the snow and ice never thaw.

In January, the coldest month, temperatures in the southern Colchis Lowland average 42°F (6°C). In July, the warmest month, the reading is 73°F (23°C). This mild climate has made the coast of the Black Sea a major vacation area. Rainfall in the western Georgia is high, reaching more than 125 inches (318 centimeters). Although rain occurs throughout the year, it is heaviest in the autumn and winter.

A woman rushes to finish her shopping during a brief rainstorm in northwestern Georgia.

The climate of eastern and southern Georgia ranges from slightly humid in the Kartalinian Plain to quite dry in the southeastern steppes. The average January temperature in Tbilisi is about 34°F (1°C), while in July readings stay at about 76°F (24°C). Rainfall decreases with distance from the Black Sea. The plain receives about 28 inches (71 cm), while the steppes get less than half that amount.

• *Cities* •

Of Georgia's 5.5 million people, more than half live in urban areas. The country has roughly 40 cities, the largest of which is the capital of Tbilisi. Other big population centers include Kutaisi, Rustavi, Sokhumi, and Batumi. Most of these cities

(Above) *Although an ancient city, Tbilisi contains a number of modern high-rise apartment buildings.* (Below) *A resident of the capital passes in front of the looping arches of a Soviet-built reviewing stand that dates to the 1980s.*

(Above) *Visitors to Sokhumi, a Georgian port on the Black Sea, enjoy one of the city's parks on a warm and sunny day.* (Below) *Suntanning is a popular activity at the beachfront in Batumi.*

were founded under Georgia's prosperous ancient kingdoms.

Tbilisi (population 1.2 million) is home to nearly one-fifth of Georgia's entire population. Lying along the banks of the Kura River, the city is protected by mountains on three sides. Founded in the 5th century A.D., Tbilisi came under Russian rule in 1801, when its name was changed to Tiflis. After the Communist revolution of 1917, Tbilisi became the seat of power of the Soviet Transcaucasian republic.

Tbilisi has long been a hub of trade between Asia and Europe. The city also was a stop on the **Silk Road**, an ancient overland trade route between China and Europe. In the 1800s and 1900s, the Russians and Soviets built factories in the capital to produce machinery, tools, electrical equipment, textiles, furniture, and wine.

Located along the Rioni River in central Georgia, Kutaisi (population 236,000) is a major industrial center that makes vehicles, mining equipment, textiles, and processed foods. In addition to its modern economic importance, Kutaisi also has a key place in Georgian history. The city, under the name Aea, was the center of ancient Colchis and later was the capital of the kingdom of Imeritia.

Rustavi (population 160,000), Georgia's third largest city, lies about 15 miles (24 km) southeast of Tbilisi. Rustavi grew because of a large metal-making plant that began to operate in the 1940s. Since then, the high quality of the factory's iron, steel, and other metal goods has become well known throughout the former Soviet Union.

The Black Sea ports of Batumi (population 137,000) and Sokhumi (population 121,000) are vital to Georgia's economy. They serve as transportation hubs for the many agricultural products raised in the region.

The administrative capital of the Georgian province of Adjara, Batumi exports Georgia's manganese ore and manufactured goods. The city's factories produce ships, machinery, and furniture and process tea and tobacco. A pipeline carrying oil from Azerbaijan ends at Batumi, where a large refinery operates. Violence in the Transcaucasus region has often interrupted incoming oil supplies and has stopped refining activities.

In peaceful times, visitors can climb the hill behind Sokhumi, the capital of Abkhazia, to get a broad view of the port, which exports wine, processed foods, and leather goods. Ferries, airlines, roads, and railways link the city to other parts of Georgia and the Black Sea region, helping to make Sokhumi a favorite vacation spot. Tourism declined in Sokhumi throughout the early 1990s, however, as armed groups of Abkhazians fought Georgia's national guard for Abkhazia's independence.

(Above) *In Kutaisi, a manufacturing hub in central Georgia, a young singer gets ready to perform.* (Below) *Georgian Orthodox believers come and go through the ornate door of Sioni Cathedral in Tbilisi.*

• Ethnic and Religious Heritage •

More than two-thirds of Georgia's population are ethnic Georgians, most of whom belong to the Georgian Orthodox Church. Adjarans are ethnic Georgians who follow the Islamic religion. The remainder of the population is made up of Armenians, Azeris, Russians, Ossetians, and Abkhazians.

Georgians accepted Christianity in the 4th century A.D., when the missionary Nino converted the king and queen of the kingdom of Iberia. This event led to the baptism of the rest of the population, and Christian churches sprang up throughout the region. Several of them still stand as evidence of the country's early adoption of the Christian faith.

By the late 5th century, the young Georgian church had established its own structure under a leader called a Catholicos. In the 11th century, when

From this minaret (tower) near Tbilisi, Islamic criers summon faithful Muslims (followers of Islam) to prayer.

Christianity split into two separate branches, the Georgian church allied itself with the Orthodox group, which also included Russian Christians. In the 1800s, the Russians took over Georgia and abolished the Georgian Orthodox Church. In the 1980s and 1990s, the revived church became a driving force in the Georgian independence movement.

Invading Arab armies first brought Islam to Georgia in the 7th century. During the period of Turkish domination of Georgia, which began in the mid-1400s, many Adjarans and Abkhazians adopted the Islamic faith of the Turks. Both of the main branches of Islam—Shiism and Sunnism—now exist in Georgia. The Azeris, like the Iranians, belong to the smaller Shiite sect. The Adjarans and Abkhazians accept the Sunni form followed by a majority of Muslims (Islamic believers).

Although Jews are not numerous in Georgia, large Jewish communities thrive in Tbilisi and Kutaisi. These cities have many Jewish synagogues and schools. Several groups of Jews live in Georgia's isolated mountainous regions.

• *Language and Literature* •

The Georgian language belongs to the Ibero-Caucasian family, which is distinct from every other language group. Written with its own alphabet, Georgian has a complex grammar that is hard to learn. Speakers of the various dialects of Georgian are not always able to understand one another. Both Russian and Soviet authorities tried to ban the use of written and spoken Georgian as a way of weakening Georgian nationalism.

Georgian is the official language, but other tongues are in use in Georgia. These include Russian—a Slavic language written in the Cyrillic alphabet—and Ossetian, which is related to Persian.

Georgia's Armenian population speaks another distinct language in the Caucasus region.

Despite Russian and Soviet attempts to stamp out Georgian culture, Georgians have treasured their language and literature as key parts of their national identity. Early Georgian writers chose religious themes, such as the lives of Georgian saints, as their subject matters. During the 12th century, the activities of a prosperous Georgian kingdom inspired Shota Rustaveli's *The Knight in the Panther's Skin*, Georgia's national epic. A lengthy romantic poem, the tale describes kidnappings, rescues, dangerous journeys, and finally the reunion of lovers.

The 19th-century poems of Nikoloz Baratashvili and Akaki Tsereteli expressed the Georgians' hopes for independence from Russian rule. Modern Georgian poets include Galaktion Tabidze and Giorgi Leonidze, whose works were strictly censored under Soviet Communism. The novelist Konstantine Gamsakhurdia authored historical works that reflected Georgia's pride in its ancient heritage. The Soviets persecuted many Georgian writers, poets, and historians for suspected disloyalty during the 1930s, 1940s, and 1950s.

• Health and Education •

Georgia has long been known for its beneficial climate, and most Georgians enjoy robust good health far into their senior years. In fact, more than 20,000 (less than 1 percent) of the nation's citizens are older than 90. Good medical facilities exist throughout the country, although in troubled areas some services may not be available. Recent civil conflicts have injured people in many cities, especially in Sokhumi, Abkhazia, and in Tskhinvali, South Ossetia.

(Above) *In an illustration from the Georgian epic* The Knight in the Panther's Skin, *three knights discuss how to scale the walls of a fortress.* (Below) *Many Georgians live longer than the national average life expectancy of 72 years.*

(Left) **Near the ancient Georgian capital of Mtskheta, a man ties strips of cloth to a tree as part of a pre-Christian ritual.** (Below) **Elementary schoolchildren are on their best behavior during a visit by U.S. guests.**

The average life expectancy at birth for a Georgian is 72 years, which is better than that of most countries in southwestern Asia. About 33 out of 1,000 Georgian babies die before their first birthday. This infant mortality rate is below the average for the region.

Education has been a high priority for Georgians for hundreds of years. The country's first schools date to the 4th century A.D., but many farm families and mountain dwellers of the time did not have access to them. The Soviets expanded the number of schools in Georgia, and attendance became compulsory. By the early 1990s, the state-run schools had taught nearly all Georgians to read and write.

The old Soviet curriculum included the teaching of Communist ideals. Since gaining independence, the country has eliminated courses in Communist doctrine and has emphasized instruction in Georgian literature and history. Most students attend eight years of basic schooling and then choose a secondary school that specializes in agriculture, medicine, education, or business.

After finishing secondary school, Georgian students can enter one of several institutions of higher learning. Among the major colleges and universities are Tbilisi State University and the Georgian Academy of Sciences. Established in 1941, the academy has about 200 research institutes that work in different fields of science. Financial cutbacks may reduce the number of the academy's institutes.

CHAPTER TWO

Georgia's Story

T he Transcaucasus region, which lies be-tween the plains of Russia and the deserts of the Middle East, has a long and turbulent history. The various kingdoms that once made up Georgia experienced invasion and conquest by Greece, Rome, Persia (modern Iran), Turkey, and Russia. Yet, these ancient Georgian realms also enjoyed long periods of prosperity and peaceful self-rule.

Archaeological evidence suggests that humans lived in what is now Georgia as early as 800,000 years ago. Fragments of household pottery show that people of the New Stone Age (about 10,000 B.C.) survived in the area by fishing and farming.

After about 3500 B.C., the peoples inhabiting western Georgia started to mine the region's cop-per, gold, and silver. Trade in these metal products led to the rise of wealthy, independent clans.

Overlooking the skyline of Tbilisi is the Narikala Fortress, which dates to the 4th century A.D., when the Persians were in control of Georgia. In the 5th century, the Georgian king Vakhtang Gorgasali added to the stronghold after making Tbilisi his capital. Destroyed many times, the fortress shows the renovations by later conquerors, including Arabs, Mongols, Turks, and Russians.

Fire-breathing dragons and other fierce, snorting beasts protect the golden fleece of King Aeetes, ruler of the ancient Georgian kingdom of Colchis. The Greek writer Euripides told the story of the adventurer Jason, who captured the fleece with the help of the king's daughter Medea.

Members of the clans buried their chieftains in above-ground graves filled with finely crafted metal goods. As the clans prospered and intermarried, they eventually formed the kingdom of Colchis. This domain of legendary riches was the home of King Aeetes whose golden fleece was described in ancient tales and histories.

• Early Invaders •

The wealth of Colchis attracted the seafaring Greeks, who colonized the western coast of Georgia by about the 7th century B.C. The Greek presence weakened the kingdom and allowed the old clans to again become self-governing. Beginning in the 6th century B.C., the clans came under the control of the Achaemenids, a family of rulers from Persia. The Greek commander Alexander the Great defeated the Achaemenids and divided the Colchian clans in the 4th century B.C. Alexander's death in 323 B.C. led to further disunity in western Georgia.

At the same time, a new realm called Iberia was emerging in central Georgia. It grew wealthy and became a formidable military power. In 65 B.C., troops from the Roman Empire swept through Colchis and Iberia. Although the Iberian army resisted, it was eventually defeated. The Romans then ruled Colchis directly from their base on the Italian Peninsula. Iberia became a Roman dependency that was governed by local leaders.

The Romans built new roads and introduced their laws and customs to the people of Georgia. The Silk Road, which passed through the Caucasus, allowed the region to prosper from trade between Asia and Europe. Caravans laden with silk fabric, spices, and other goods arrived at Georgia's Black Sea ports and continued on to the Middle East and the Mediterranean.

Political infighting and hostile invasions caused the decline and division of the Roman Empire in the 4th century A.D. The Western Roman Empire remained centered in Rome. The Eastern Roman (or Byzantine) Empire, which controlled western Georgia and Iberia, had its capital at Byzantium (modern Istanbul, Turkey).

Meanwhile, people throughout the crumbling empire were accepting Christianity, a faith that had its roots in the Middle East. According to Georgian tradition, a Christian woman named Nino converted the king, queen, and population of Iberia to the new religion, which eventually spread to other parts of the Caucasus.

Becoming a Christian nation put Georgia in a dangerous position, however. The Persians, who followed a different faith, sought control of the region's wealth and strategically located ports. But the Byzantine Empire, whose leaders were Christians, wished to maintain its hold on Georgia. As a result, Georgia became the battleground of two opposing powers.

A monument in Tbilisi honors King Vakhtang Gorgasali, who founded the city on the spot where, according to legend, he shot a deer while on a hunting expedition. The bleeding animal fell into a warm, underground spring and was healed of its wound. After examining the bubbling spring, the king also found the warm water healthful and ordered a settlement to be built on the site.

• Georgian Kingdoms •

In the 5th century, the Iberian king Vakhtang Gorgasali declared self-rule and set up Tbilisi as his capital, but the Persians crushed the independence movement and dismantled the monarchy. For about 200 years, local leaders called *eristavs* governed the Georgian people, who lived without a central authority.

The disunited Georgians were no match for the Arab armies that invaded in the mid-7th century. Bringing the new religion of Islam, the Arabs overthrew the eristavs and set up an emirate (an Islamic province) in Tbilisi. The Arabs governed their far-flung empire with the help of local aristocrats. This practice permitted new dynasties (families of rulers) to emerge in western and eastern Georgia.

By the late 10th century, the noble family of the Bagratids ruled Georgia. In 1008, through marriage alliances and negotiation, Bagrat III united the eastern and western realms into a single Georgian kingdom. Tbilisi remained an Arab emirate until 1122, when the Bagratid king David the Builder captured the city and ended Arab authority in Georgia. A successful commander and administrator, David seized large sections of what is now Armenia and reformed the Georgian code of laws. A patron of the arts, he left a stable and well-run kingdom to his successors.

Georgia enjoyed a golden age in the late 12th and early 13th centuries during the reign of Queen Tamara. Sensible laws and wise foreign policy en-

These stone details from Sveti-tskhoveli Cathedral, also called the Church of the Pillar of Life, date from the 11th century, when the cathedral was substantially remodeled. Originally constructed in Mtskheta in the 4th century, the church hosted the coronations and burials of several Georgian kings.

The monogram of Queen Tamara, written in ancient lettering, appeared on the coinage from her reign, which lasted from 1184 to 1212.

(Right) **The Church of the Assumption in the town of Vardzia features many frescoes (paintings on plaster), including these portraits of Queen Tamara and her father, King Giorgi III.** (Below) **The Georgian poet Shota Rustaveli wrote his masterpiece** The Knight in the Panther's Skin *during Tamara's period of rule.*

sured the stability of the kingdom, which extended from Azerbaijan in the east to southern Russia in the west. Tamara's court welcomed poets, painters, and musicians, including Shota Rustaveli, who dedicated *The Knight in the Panther's Skin* to the queen.

This period of prosperity ended abruptly in about 1220, when large armies of Mongol warriors invaded Transcaucasia from the east. The conquerors looted cities, destroyed farms, and massacred populations. The actions of the Mongols, who ended centralized power in Georgia, ruined the area's thriving economy.

In the early 1400s, after the Mongols had abandoned the region, Queen Tamara's successors organized the Georgian kingdom into three Bagratid princedoms. The senior branch of the family ruled Kartli from its capital in Tbilisi. A second Bagratid line controlled Imeritia in western Georgia. The kingdom of Kakheti was the easternmost Bagratid holding.

• Turkish and Persian Influence •

In 1453, the Ottoman Turks captured Constantinople, the capital of the Byzantine Empire. The Turks, who followed the Islamic religion, sacked Tbilisi and Kutaisi and converted some groups in western Georgia to Islam. The Turkish invasion cut off Kartli, Imeritia, and Kakheti from Christian nations in Europe.

The Persians also had territorial designs on Georgia, which eventually was divided into Turkish and Persian spheres of influence. The Ottoman Turks controlled the ports of western Georgia, which still profited from trade. The Persians governed Kakheti and Kartli, from which the Persian shah (ruler) Abbas I deported thousands of Georgians in the late 16th and early 17th centuries. The Bagratids in Imeritia managed to resist the Turks, but the Bagratid princes in Kartli and Kakheti ruled only with the approval of the shah.

Caught between Turkey and Persia, the Georgian princedoms sought help from Russia, a powerful Christian empire to the north. Prince Vakhtang VI, who reigned over Kartli and Kakheti in the early 18th century, supported the Russian czar (ruler) Peter the Great who fought unsuccessfully to eliminate Persia's presence from Transcaucasia.

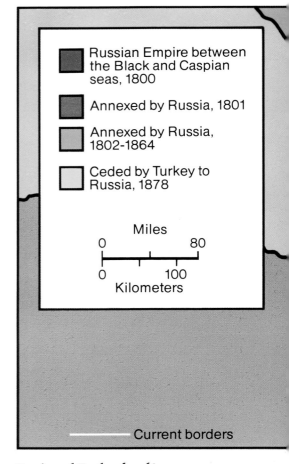

Russian Empire between the Black and Caspian seas, 1800

Annexed by Russia, 1801

Annexed by Russia, 1802-1864

Ceded by Turkey to Russia, 1878

Miles
0   80

0   100
Kilometers

——— Current borders

Persia and Turkey fought over the Caucasus region from the 15th to the 18th centuries. Meanwhile, another power—the Russian Empire—began to push southward into the same area. This map shows Russia's annexations (takeovers) of Georgian territory in the 19th century.

Vakhtang's successor Erekle II also allied with the Russian Empire. In 1783, Erekle and the czarina Catherine the Great signed the Treaty of Georgiyevsk. The agreement guaranteed the existence of the Georgian monarchy in exchange for accepting Russia's supreme authority. But when the Persian army attacked Kartli in 1795, the Russians did nothing to defend the Georgian realm.

Weakened by the Persian invasion, Kartli and Kakheti soon fell prey to the Russians, who **annexed** (took over) them in 1801 and went on to capture Imeritia in 1810. Throughout the 19th century, the czars used their armies to seize Georgian land until the entire region was under Russian control.

Modernized by the Russians in the early 1800s, the Georgian Military Highway stretches from Ordzhonikidze, the capital of North Ossetia, to Tbilisi. A large manual labor force and powerful explosives widened the rugged overland link across the Greater Caucasus Mountains.

• *Georgia under the Russians* •

The Russians made many changes in their attempt to **Russify** Georgia. They abolished the Georgian Orthodox Church, for example, and replaced the traditional Georgian administration with a Russian-style bureaucracy. The Georgian language and Georgian literature were suppressed. These actions ignited many popular revolts, and Georgia became known as a nationalistic region strongly opposed to czarist rule.

At the same time, the Russians developed the Georgian economy and transportation system. A railway linked Poti and Tbilisi in 1872. Foreign investment led to the opening or expansion of mines, factories, and agricultural estates. The Russians built schools to broaden education, and Tbilisi became a cultural hub in Transcaucasia.

Throughout the late 1800s and early 1900s, many Georgians joined anti-czarist organizations. Prince Ilya Chavchavadze headed the Pirveli Dasi, or First Group, which sought peaceful change and the restoration of the Georgian language and traditions. More radical programs came from the Meore Dasi (Second Group) and the Mesame Dasi (Third Group). Joseph Dzhugashvili, later known as Stalin, was one of the founders of the Third Group, which followed Communist ideals.

Czarist troops routinely put down nationalist protests in Georgia in the early 1900s. Public demonstrations, particularly by Communist political activists, were also causing turmoil in other parts of the Russian Empire. Meanwhile, an international conflict was brewing. The empire's alliances with Britain and France pushed the czar's forces into World War I (1914–1918) against Austria, Germany, and Turkey.

Born in the mountain town of Gori, Joseph Stalin (pictured here in 1913) *was a good student who won a scholarship to attend a seminary in Tbilisi. The harsh routine of the religious school helped to form some of Stalin's revolutionary ideas, which he applied with ruthless energy after becoming the Soviet Union's leader in the late 1920s.*

• **Soviet Rule** •

In 1917, as Russia was experiencing defeat on the battlefield, the Communists staged an antigovernment revolt that eventually toppled the czar. A committee of Russian Communists organized Georgia, Armenia, and Azerbaijan into a federation, but a Turkish invasion caused the federation to break up. Georgians seized the opportunity to declare their independence and to set up a self-ruling state in May 1918.

Georgian independence did not last, however. The forces of the Communist Red Army invaded in 1921. By 1922, the Communists had founded the Union of Soviet Socialist Republics (USSR). It included the Transcaucasian Soviet Federated Socialist Republic, which was made up of Georgia, Armenia, and Azerbaijan.

Stalin, who became the Soviet leader in the late 1920s, viewed Georgian nationalism as a threat to the USSR. He authorized the execution of Georgian activists, restricted the work of the Georgian Orthodox Church, and jailed intellectuals and professionals. Although these actions caused unrest, the Red Army stamped out Georgian opposition. The Soviet secret police, headed by another Georgian named Lavrenty Beria, also persecuted and executed Georgians who criticized Stalin's policies.

At the same time, Stalin aimed to industrialize Georgia and other parts of the Soviet Union. He ordered the building of new Georgian factories and

A billboard in Tbilisi displays the flags of the 15 states that made up the Union of Soviet Socialist Republics.

Under Stalin's rule, Georgia's agricultural sector was upgraded, and farms were combined into large estates. Nevertheless, much of the planting and harvesting was still done by hand. Here, tea pickers take a break from their labors.

expanded the region's educational and health systems. During the 1930s, the Soviets forcibly combined many of Georgia's agricultural holdings into **collective farms.** On these state-owned properties, the harvest was turned over to the government, which set prices, controlled distribution, and paid workers a fixed salary. In 1936, a new Soviet constitution dismantled the Transcaucasian republic and established the Georgian Soviet Socialist Republic (SSR).

• *World War II and Its Aftermath* •

Soviet Georgia contributed soldiers, food, and manufactured goods during World War II (1939–1945), another international conflict that pitted the Soviet Union and its allies against Germany. In 1941, after the Germans launched a surprise attack on the western USSR, Georgian military units stopped German troops from overrunning the northern Caucasus. Soviet Georgia was thus spared the destruction that occurred in Russia and other western Soviet republics.

Stalin's repressive policies continued during the war. Distrusting Soviet Georgia's ethnic minorities, he ordered the deportation of Meskhetian Turks and Chechen-Ingush to the eastern USSR. After the war, thousands of Georgians lost their jobs—and even their lives—through accusations of disloyalty to Stalin and the Communist party. Many Georgian writers, intellectuals, scientists, and politicians were executed during the **purges** of the 1940s and 1950s.

After Stalin died in 1953, Soviet repression eased in the Georgian SSR. His successor, Nikita Khrushchev, denounced Stalin's harsh and destructive policies. This declaration was not entirely popular with the Georgian people, many of whom were proud of Stalin's influence in international affairs.

Throughout the 1960s and 1970s, Soviet Georgia's economy strengthened. Newly built hydropower stations supplied energy to factories that produced iron and steel goods and to mines that extracted coal and manganese ore. Collectives in the Colchis Lowland provided tea, fruits, and tobacco to markets throughout the Soviet Union. Yet Georgians struggled with shortages of housing, food, and consumer goods. Soviet leaders still restricted the freedom to worship, to publish, or to criticize the government. Many ethnic Georgians were dissatisfied with Soviet rule, and the republic's ethnic minorities began to campaign for more rights.

Stalin's fall from grace after his death in 1953 did not please all Georgians. This resident of the mining town of Akhaltsikhe, for example, saved an old portrait of the Georgian-born Soviet dictator.

• **Recent Events** •

By 1985, when the Soviet leader Mikhail Gorbachev came to power, republics throughout the USSR were experiencing worsening economic and social problems. In response, Gorbachev introduced two new policies—***glasnost*** (meaning ''openness'') and ***perestroika*** (meaning ''restructuring'').

Graffiti that proclaimed the underground popularity of British and U.S. rock groups appeared in the 1980s, after Mikhail Gorbachev introduced **glasnost**, *a policy that loosened restrictions on freedom of expression.*

Glasnost allowed Georgians and other Soviet citizens to talk more openly about Soviet programs, and perestroika permitted new methods of running factories, farms, and mines. A strong supporter of Gorbachev's reforms was Soviet Georgia's Communist party leader Eduard Shevardnadze, who became the USSR's foreign minister in 1985.

(Right) *A young boy waves the flag of the independent Republic of Georgia.* (Below) *In the early 1990s, frequent fighting in Abkhazia brought out the Georgian national guard, which battled Abkhazia's minority Muslim population for control of the province.*

By 1989, the citizens of the Georgian SSR were testing the limits of glasnost. Abkhazians and South Ossetians campaigned to secede from (leave) the republic. Ethnic Georgians in Abkhazia and elsewhere in Soviet Georgia strongly opposed Abkhazian and South Ossetian self-rule. An anti-secession demonstration in Tbilisi turned violent when Soviet soldiers fired on participants, killing 20 and injuring many others. The incident increased anti-Soviet feelings in the Georgian SSR and worsened turmoil among the republic's ethnic groups.

In 1990 and 1991, the Georgian parliament, which included some non-Communists, took its first steps toward independence. It dropped the words "Soviet" and "Socialist" from the country's name and reintroduced the white, black, and maroon flag used by the independent Georgian government of 1918. The parliament also declared it illegal for the Soviet Union to draft Georgians into the Red Army. Many young people instead joined the Georgian national guard.

After a majority of Georgians voted in support of independence, the parliament declared the restoration of Georgian self-rule and established the office of executive president. In national elections held in May 1991, Zviad Gamsakhurdia, a well-known anti-Communist and the son of a famous Georgian writer, won the presidency with more than 85 percent of the vote. Within a few months,

Burned buildings in Tbilisi are grim reminders of the anti-government rioting that erupted in the city in January 1992.

however, Gamsakhurdia had made himself extremely unpopular among Georgians. He fired ministers who disagreed with him, jailed opposition leaders, and ordered the use of force against demonstrators in Tbilisi, Abkhazia, and South Ossetia.

Political unrest was also occurring in other Soviet republics. The turmoil alarmed conservative Communist politicians and military leaders, who tried to overthrow Gorbachev in a **coup d'état** in August 1991. This event split the Georgian leadership between Gamsakhurdia, who was slow to condemn the plot, and those who wanted to restore Gorbachev to power. After the coup failed, demonstrators and politicians, including Shevardnadze, demanded Gamsakhurdia's resignation.

As other republics followed Georgia's example and declared their independence, Gorbachev lost control of the USSR. By December, some of the seceding republics had formed the Commonwealth of Independent States, an association of former SSRs that Georgia did not join. In January 1992, after months of riots, shootings, and violent demonstrations, Gamsakhurdia fled the country.

A state council, headed by Shevardnadze, eventually took over the Georgian government until national elections were held in October 1992. Shevardnadze won overwhelming support as leader of the Georgian parliament. Since then, he has worked to restore stability to the region.

Nevertheless, fighting continues in Abkhazia and South Ossetia, and Russian troops stationed in Georgia before the USSR's breakup have been involved in the conflicts. The secession movement in these provinces has increased tensions between the Russian and Georgian governments. In addition, the Georgian economy is in ruins, and food is scarce. These problems make Georgia's future complicated and far from certain.

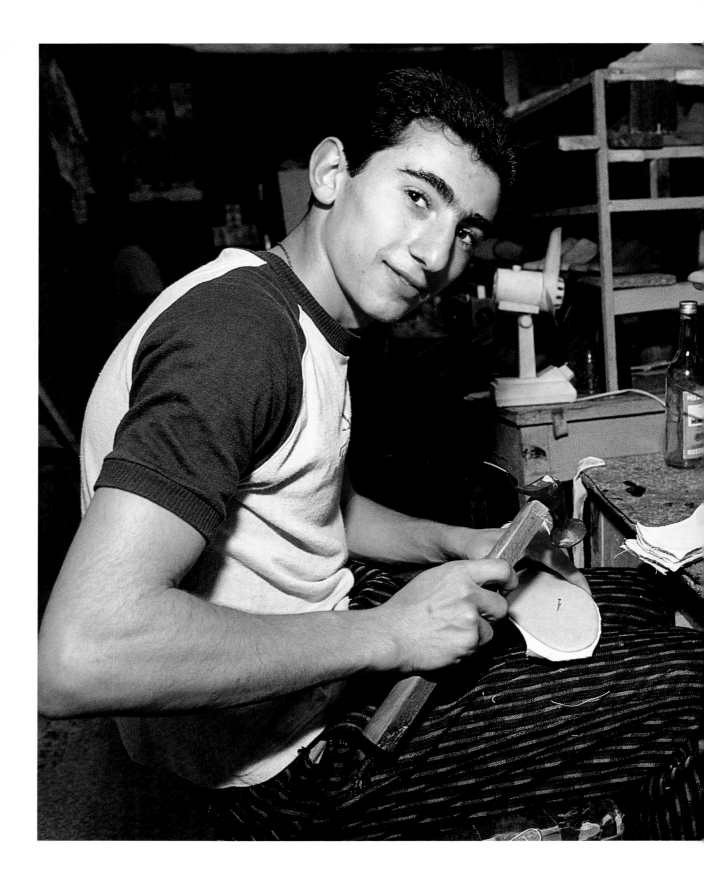

CHAPTER THREE

Making a Living in Georgia

T he Georgian economy has seen many ups and downs during the 20th century. After the Soviet annexation, the output of mines and factories dropped. Beginning in the late 1920s, however, the Soviets increased investment in Soviet Georgia to take advantage of its many natural resources. Newly built hydroelectric power plants provided energy to a growing list of industries, including an oil refinery, textile mills, and plants that processed tea and tobacco.

After World War II, Soviet Georgia's economy expanded on a grand scale. Huge hydropower stations began to operate, and large factories assembled vehicles, engines, machinery, and metal goods. Expanded railways, roads, and ferry lines served the busy ports at Batumi, Sokhumi, Gagra, and Poti.

Using glue and nails, a shoemaker in Tbilisi molds pieces of leather to wooden lasts (foot-shaped forms).

Since independence, political instability has again hampered Georgia's economy. There is a shortage of cash, and foreign investors are wary of putting money in Georgian businesses. Soaring inflation rates, a decline in industrial production, and rising food prices have hurt the standard of living for most Georgians.

The government is now making economic reforms. It is selling some state-operated businesses to private owners and is also seeking investment from abroad, especially from Iran. Yet, the move from a state-controlled economy to a free-market system amid civil unrest is proving extremely difficult.

• Agriculture and Forestry •

Georgian farmers harvest a broad range of cash crops, but a shortage of flat, arable land prevents the raising of grain or livestock on a large scale. Western Georgia—which enjoys both ample sunshine

Among Georgia's most valued crops are tea (left) *and wine grapes* (above), *both of which are often gathered by hand.*

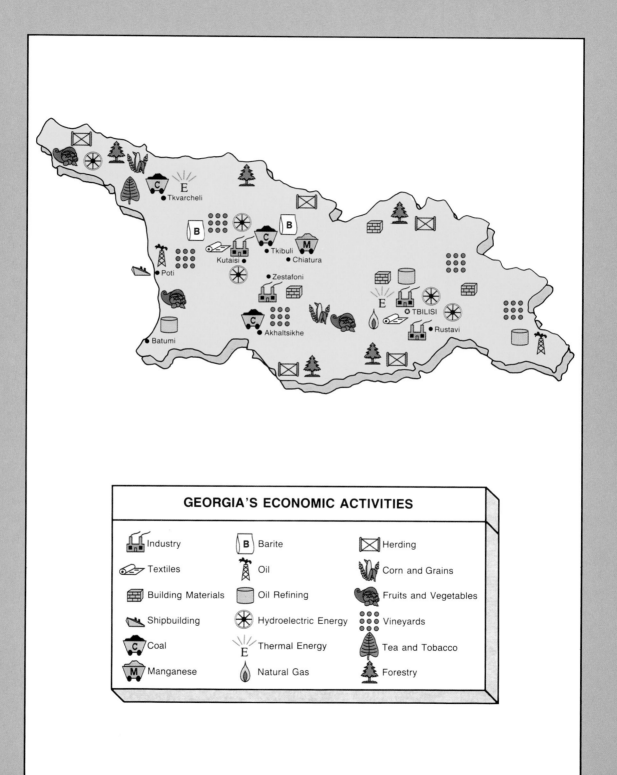

GEORGIA'S ECONOMIC ACTIVITIES

Industry	**B** Barite	Herding
Textiles	Oil	Corn and Grains
Building Materials	Oil Refining	Fruits and Vegetables
Shipbuilding	Hydroelectric Energy	Vineyards
C Coal	**E** Thermal Energy	Tea and Tobacco
M Manganese	Natural Gas	Forestry

In southern Georgia, a shepherd guides his flock to pasture.

and plentiful rainfall—produces tea, oranges, tangerines, lemons, pomegranates, corn, tobacco, and sugar beets. Slightly inland, farmers cultivate grapes, which are crushed and aged to make brandies, wines, and champagnes. Flowering plants, such as jasmines, geraniums, and roses, are processed into oils for the perfume industry.

The Kartalinian Plain and irrigated areas farther east are prime land for the growing of grapes, which is an age-old occupation in the region. Over the centuries, Georgian farmers have established more than 500 varieties of grapes. Farms in the plain also cultivate grains, vegetables, and noncitrus fruits. Mountainous areas offer winter and summer pasture for sheep, goats, and cattle, and some farms raise pigs and poultry.

Forests cover about 30 percent of Georgia's land. Tung trees, which thrive along the western coasts, yield an oil that is refined into a waterproofing and painting chemical. Mulberry trees line the banks of many rivers in western Georgia. The leaves

Most of Georgia's deposits of manganese ore lie near Chiatura. Powerful, motor-driven shovels remove the soil to uncover the manganese, which is then broken up and loaded onto trucks. To restore the land after the mining operation is finished, miners return the soil to its previous location.

of this species are the main food of silkworms, whose finely spun cocoons are processed into raw silk fabric. Evergreen and deciduous (leaf-shedding) forests that exist in the Greater and Lesser Caucasus mountains supply a small woodworking industry.

• Mining and Energy •

Despite Georgia's small size, the country is rich in mineral and energy resources. Chiatura, near Kutaisi, has large, easily accessible deposits of manganese ore, which is processed into high-grade steel alloys. Stocks of black and brown coal at Tkibuli, Tkvarcheli, and Akhaltsikhe meet some of the country's energy demands. Western Georgia also has substantial supplies of barite, a substance that is used in making dyes and X-ray films.

Central and eastern Georgia contain deposits of building stone and other materials that are needed by the construction industry. Experts regard the fine marble from the mountains of eastern Georgia to be equal in quality to the more famous varieties from Italy and Greece.

Small supplies of oil exist in western and eastern Georgia. Pipelines bring additional crude oil from Azerbaijan to the refinery at Batumi. Natural gas from western Azerbaijan also travels via pipeline to Tbilisi and then northward to Russia. Fighting in Azerbaijan has cut off incoming oil and natural gas more than once in recent years. Agreements reached in late 1992 may extend the natural-gas pipeline to Iran.

The Soviets developed hydropower in Georgia by building several stations on the Kura, Inguri, and Rioni rivers. These plants provide hydroelectricity to industries in Tbilisi, Rustavi, and Kutaisi. Thermal plants—fired by either coal or natural gas—operate near Tkvarcheli and Tbilisi.

HYDROPOWER'S HANG-UPS

Fossil fuels, such as coal and petroleum, supply Georgia with most of its energy. In recent years, the country has also developed hydropower, which uses the force of falling water to create electricity. Hydroelectric dams now operate on the Inguri, Rioni, and Kura rivers.

Most hydroelectric dams hold river water in large, elevated storage spaces known as a reservoirs. The water falls through a tunnel in the dam, hitting the blades of a huge wheel called a turbine. The force of the water turns the turbine, which is linked to an electric generator. Power lines hooked to the generator deliver electricity to homes and industries. The turbine can also pump river water back into the reservoir for reuse.

Hydropower has several advantages over fossil fuels. It is non-polluting and renewable—meaning that it can be reused over again. Burning fossil fuels, on the other hand, produces poisonous fumes, and these fuels can be used up.

But hydropower still has its drawbacks. To create reservoirs, engineers flood the land, sometimes destroying farms, villages, and natural habitats for plants and animals. In large reservoirs, storms can produce waves that wear away the surrounding land. The still water held by reservoirs can become the breeding place for insects that are harmful to people and crops.

These disadvantages have made many Georgians rethink the decision to build large hydropower stations. Some of the country's environmentalists believe that smaller, more efficient dams may lessen flooding and may save Georgia's limited farmland and natural habitats.

Constructed in the 1980s, the hydropower station on the Inguri River lies high in mountains of northwestern Georgia.

(Left) **Using the wool from locally raised sheep, a weaver in Tbilisi produces a section of carpet.** (Below) **Workers at an assembly plant in Kutaisi put the finishing touches on the cabs of new trucks.**

• Industry •

Although expanded in the 20th century, Georgia's industries need to be modernized to be able to compete on the world market. A lack of investment is slowing efforts to upgrade equipment and to streamline the distribution of goods.

Metal-making factories at Rustavi and Zestafoni—now among Georgia's most important businesses—forge high-grade sheet iron and seamless steel pipes that are known throughout the old Soviet Union. Industrial complexes in Tbilisi and Kutaisi produce a variety of heavy machinery and vehicles, including trucks, cars, locomotives, farm equipment, construction vehicles, and tools.

Georgians also run specialized textile and food industries. Locally raised sheep and silkworms supply wool and silk factories with raw materials. Companies that make red and white table wines, dessert wines, brandies, and champagnes depend on Georgia's many vineyards. Georgia's emphasis on farming has led to the expansion of the chemical industry to include agricultural fertilizers, as well as medicines and artificial fibers. Local stone and cement help to supply building companies with slate, concrete, and prefabricated materials.

What's Next for Georgia?

T hroughout the 20th century, Georgians yearned for independence, even as the Russian and Soviet governments built up Georgia's industries and expanded its agriculture. Self-rule has been achieved, but the cost has been high. Zviad Gamsakhurdia's strict and violent regime showed Georgians that authoritarian rule can come from anywhere, even from a popular anti-Communist who won election by a huge majority.

The Shevardnadze administration permits freedom of speech and welcomes opposition groups into the political process. Using his experience as the Soviet foreign minister, Shevardnadze

Georgian teenagers pause outside the door of Svetitskhoveli Cathedral in the historic town of Mtskheta.

INTERNATIONAL WORD GUIDE
ver. 2.1

ENGLISH	GEORGIAN	PRONUNCIATION
Georgia	საქართველო	sakar-tveh-lo
Hello	გამარჯობა	gah-mar-dj-obah
Goodbye	ნახვამდის	na-khvam-dis
Please	გეთაყვა(ნე)	geta-kva-nee
Thank you	მადლობა||ა	mahd-lo-bah
Yes	კი	kee
No	არ(ა)	arah
Good	კარგი||ი	kar-gee
Bad	ავ||ი	avee

has been able to bring Georgia into the international community by establishing diplomatic relations with many nations, including the United States, Turkey, Iran, and Britain. He also wants to enact reforms that will put the Georgian economy on the road to recovery.

Despite these achievements, ongoing civil war, ethnic tension, and religious division are slowing Georgia's search for political stability. In addition,

At a cafe attached to a small health resort, a waitress brings patrons their order of bread and cheese. With its mild climate, Georgia has great potential as a vacation spot, but ongoing unrest discourages most visitors.

Russia has used its soldiers and influence to interfere in Abkhazia and South Ossetia—a development that threatens war between the two nations. Although Georgia has tremendous economic potential, little real progress can take place until the country is at peace, until its borders are stable, and until its people believe that the government is working for the good of all the nation's citizens.

FAST FACTS ABOUT GEORGIA

Total Population	5.5 million
Ethnic Mixture	69 percent Georgian 9 percent Armenian 7 percent Russian 5 percent Azeri 3 percent Ossetian 2 percent Abkhazian
CAPITAL and Major Cities	TBILISI, Kutaisi, Rustavi, Batumi, Sokhumi
Major Languages	Georgian, Russian
Major Religions	Georgian Orthodox, Islam (Sunni branch)
Year of Inclusion in USSR	1936
Status	Fully independent state; member of United Nations since July 1992; ongoing fighting for self-rule in Abkhazia and South Ossetia

annex: to add a country or territory to the domain of another by force.

collective farm: a large agricultural estate worked by a group. The workers usually received a portion of the farm's harvest as wages. On a Soviet collective farm, the central government owned the land, buildings, and machinery.

Commonwealth of Independent States: a union of former Soviet republics that was created in December 1991. The commonwealth has no formal constitution and functions as a loose economic and military association. Georgia is not a member.

Communist: a person who supports Communism—an economic system in which the government owns all farmland and the means of producing goods in factories.

A tapestry depicting traditional Georgian dancers adorns the wall of a Tbilisi restaurant.

Pastel colors decorate a shop-front in the old part of the capital.

An illustration from **The Knight in the Panther's Skin** *shows one of the heroes meeting his lover for the first time.*

coup d'état: French words meaning "blow to the state" that refer to a swift, sudden overthrow of a government.

ethnic Georgian: a person whose ethnic heritage is Caucasian and who speaks Georgian.

glasnost: the Russian word for openness that refers to a Soviet policy of the 1980s that eased restrictions on writing and speaking.

industrialize: to build and modernize factories for the purpose of manufacturing a wide variety of consumer goods and machinery.

From the height of Mount Mtatsminda in Tbilisi, climbers can view the pale towers of St. David's Church. Originally constructed in the 1500s, the church was completely rebuilt in the late 1800s. Nearby are the graves of famous Georgian writers and activists, including Galaktion Tabidze, Nikoloz Baratashvili, and Ilya Chavchavadze.

perestroika: a policy of economic restructuring introduced in the late 1980s. Under perestroika, the Soviet state loosened its control of industry and agriculture and allowed small, private businesses to operate.

purge: the removal of people suspected of disloyalty from a group or organization.

Russian Empire: a large kingdom ruled by czars that covered present-day Russia as well as areas to the west and south. It existed from roughly the mid-1500s to 1917.

Russify: to make Russian by imposing the Russian language and culture on non-Russian peoples.

Silk Road: an ancient trade route that passed through central and southwestern Asia, linking eastern Asia with the Middle East and Europe.

Transcaucasian republic: one of the three southwest Asian republics of Georgia, Armenia, and Azerbaijan that were once part of the USSR and that have the Caucasus Mountains crossing their territories.

Union of Soviet Socialist Republics (USSR): a large nation in eastern Europe and northern Asia that consisted of 15 member-republics. It existed from 1922 to 1991.

United Nations: an international organization formed after World War II whose primary purpose is to promote world peace through discussion and cooperation.

Abkhazia, 8, 12, 20, 22, 38–39, 51

Adjara, 12, 20

Agriculture and livestock, 7, 13, 17, 19, 32, 35, 42, 44, 47

Architecture, 10–11, 18

Armenia, 11–12, 28, 33

Asia, 7, 11, 19, 23, 27

Azerbaijan, 11–12, 17, 20, 29, 33, 45

Bagrat III, 28

Batumi, 16, 18–20, 41, 45

Black Sea, 11–13, 16–19, 27

Caspian Sea, 16–17

Chavchavadze, Prince Ilya, 33, 54

Cities and towns, 8, 13, 17–20, 29, 33, 36, 41, 45, 47. See also Batumi; Kutaisi; Mtskheta; Poti; Rustavi; Sokhumi; Tbilisi

Climate, 17–18, 22

Colchis (kingdom), 19, 26

Commonwealth of Independent States, 9, 39

Communists, 7–9, 19, 22–23, 33, 36–37, 39

David the Builder, 28

Demonstrations and riots, 6–9, 32–33, 38–39. See also Welfare and civil unrest

Dzhugashvili, Joseph. See Stalin, Joseph

Economy, 8–9, 19, 30, 32, 36, 39, 41–47, 50–51

Education, 23, 32, 35

Energy, 16–17, 36, 41, 45, 46

Environmental concerns, 46

Erekle II, 31

Ethnic groups, 8–9, 11, 20–21, 36

Europe, 7, 19, 27, 30

Exports, 20

Food, 39, 42, 47

Forests, 44–45

Gamsakhurdia, Zviad, 9, 38–39, 49

Georgia
    boundaries, size, and location of, 11–12
    flag of, 38
    government of, 9, 12, 32, 38–39, 42, 49–51
    population of, 18

Georgian Soviet Socialist Republic, 35–36, 38

Georgiyevsk, Treaty of, 31

Germany, 33, 35

Gorbachev, Mikhail, 9, 37, 39

Health care, 22–23, 35

History, 8–9, 19, 21–23, 25–39, 49
    ancient, 23, 25–27
    early foreign rule, 21, 27–31
    independence, 8–9, 23, 27, 33, 38–39, 49
    Russian rule, 19, 22, 31–33
    Soviet rule, 8, 33–36

Hydropower. See Energy

Iberia, 20, 26–27

Imeritia, 19, 30–31

Signs in Georgian and other languages announce an international folk festival.

Independence, 8–9, 23, 27, 33, 38–39, 49

Industry, 7, 17, 19–20, 32, 34–36, 41–42, 44–45, 47

Inguri River, 13, 16, 45, 46

Iran, 42, 45, 50. *See also* Persia

Irrigation, 13, 16–17, 44

Jobs, 5, 36, 40–41, 47

Kakheti, 30–31

Kartli, 11, 30–31

Knight in the Panther's Skin, The, 22, 29, 53

Kura River, 16–17, 19, 45, 46

Kutaisi, 16, 18–21, 30, 45, 47

Languages, 21–22, 32–33, 50, 55

Literature, 22–23, 29, 32, 54 *See also Knight in the Panther's Skin, The*

Manufacturing. *See* Industry

Maps and charts, 14–15, 30–31, 43, 50, 51

Middle East, 25, 27

Mining, 25, 32, 36, 41, 44–45

Mountains, 11–13, 16–17, 32, 45.

Mtkvari River. *See* Kura River

Mtskheta, 13, 23, 28, 48–49

Natural resources, 20, 41, 45, 46

Nino, 20, 27

North Ossetia, 12, 32

People, 8–9, 11, 20–23, 27–28, 30, 32–33, 35–36, 38–39, 50, 55

Persia, 25–26, 30–31. *See also* Iran

Poti, 16, 32, 41

Red Army, 33–34, 38

Religion, 8, 20–23, 27–28, 30, 32, 34, 50, 54

Republics, former Soviet, 35, 37, 39. *See also* Armenia; Azerbaijan; Russia

Rioni River, 13, 16, 19, 45, 46

Rivers, 13, 16–17, 45, 46. *See also* Inguri River; Kura River; Rioni River

Roman Empire, 26–27

Rome, 25–27

Russia, 11–12, 17, 25, 29–31, 33, 35, 45, 51

Russian Empire, 7, 30–31, 33

Rustaveli, Shota, 22, 29. *See also Knight in the Panther's Skin, The*

Rustavi, 18–19, 45, 47

Shevardnadze, Eduard, 7, 9, 37, 39, 49–50

Silk Road, 19, 27

Sokhumi, 18–20, 22, 41

South Ossetia, 12, 22, 38–39, 51

Soviet Union, 7–9, 19, 33–36, 47

Stalin, Joseph, 33–36

Tamara, Queen, 28–30

Tbilisi, 6–7, 9–11, 16–21, 24–25, 27–28, 30, 32, 34, 38–41, 45, 47, 52, 54

Topography, 12–17

Tourism, 17, 19–20, 51

Trade, 19, 25, 27, 30

Transcaucasia, 29–30, 32

Transcaucasian republics, 12, 19, 33, 35

Transportation, 19–20, 32, 41

Turkey, 11, 17, 25, 27, 30–31, 33, 50

Union of Soviet Socialist Republics (USSR). *See* Soviet Union

United Nations, 9

Vakhtang Gorgasali, 25, 27

Vakhtang VI, Prince, 30–31

Warfare and civil unrest, 12, 20, 22, 25–28, 30–31, 33–36, 39, 50

• *Photo Acknowledgments* •

Photos are used courtesy of: pp. 1, 18 (bottom), 39, © Yury Tatarinov; p. 2, © Threadgill; pp. 5, 9, 18 (top), 38 (top), 44, 53 (left), © Craig Line; pp. 6, 33, NOVOSTI / SOVFOTO; pp. 8 (left), 38 (bottom), ITAR-TASS / SOVFOTO; p. 8 (right), Perry Schwartz; p. 10, Dr. Paul J. Magnarella; pp. 12 (left), 16, 32, RIA-NOVOSTI / SOVFOTO; pp. 12 (right), 42 (right), 45, 46, 47 (bottom), TASS / SOVFOTO; p. 13, Michael Hamburger; pp. 16 (bottom), 19 (top and bottom), 20 (top), 29 (right), 35, 36, 40, 42 (left), 47 (top), 55, © Jeffrey J. Foxx / NYC; pp. 17, 22 (bottom), 23 (top), 28 (right), 48, 51, 54, © Jack Corn; p. 20 (bottom), Naomi Duguid / Asia Access; p. 21, © Dennis Noonan; pp. 22 (top), 29 (left), 53 (right), Independent Picture Service; p. 23 (bottom), Ken Hawkins / Stock South; pp. 24, 34, 52, © Eugene G. Schulz; p. 26, Bettmann Archive; pp. 27, 37, Steve Latimer. Maps and charts: pp. 14–15, 43, J. Michael Roy; pp. 28 (left), 30–31, 50, 51, Laura Westlund.

Covers: (Front) © Jack Corn; (Back) © Jeffrey J. Foxx / NYC